Well Made, Fair Trade

My
SMARTPHONE
and Other Digital Accessories

CRABTREE
Publishing Company
www.crabtreebooks.com

Crabtree Publishing Company
www.crabtreebooks.com
1-800-387-7650

Published in Canada
Crabtree Publishing
616 Welland Avenue
St. Catharines, ON
L2M 5V6

Published in the United States
Crabtree Publishing
PMB 59051
350 Fifth Ave, 59th Floor
New York, NY 10118

Author: Helen Greathead

Editorial director: Kathy Middleton

Editors: Julia Bird, and Ellen Rodger

Designer: Q2A Media

Proofreader: Wendy Scavuzzo

Prepress technician: Margaret Amy Salter

Print and production coordinator: Katherine Berti

Published by Crabtree Publishing Company in 2017

First published in 2014 by Franklin Watts
(A division of Hachette Children's Books)
Copyright © Franklin Watts 2014

Photographs:
Cover: Photobuay, Darrin Henry, Umberto Shtanzman, Jeka, Barone Firenze, Chaoss, AdrianNunez, Queezz/Shutterstock.
Back Cover: NorGal/Shutterstock. Title Page: (T) Solarseven/Shutterstock; (B) Peshkova/Shutterstock. Imprint Page: Oleksiy Mark/Shutterstock. P4: Nmedia/Shutterstock; P5: Ekler/Shutterstock; P6: Bakalusha/Shutterstock; P7(T): Maxx Studio/Shutterstock; P7(B): Tong chuwit/Shutterstock; P8: Fairphone; P9: Bloomberg/Contributer/Getty Images; P10: Goodluz/Shutterstock; P11(L): TongChuwit/Shutterstock; P11(R): E+/Getty Images; P12(T): Nager-IT; P12(B): Lucas Oleniuk/Zuma Press/Corbis; P13(B): Erni/Shutterstock; P13(TL): Q2A Media; P13(TR): Ecovative Design; P14(B): Darrin Henry/Shutterstock; P15: BartlomiejMagierowski/Shutterstock; P16(C): Dmitry Kalinovsky/Shutterstock; P16(B): BartlomiejMagierowski/Shutterstock; P17: Nokia; P18(TL): David Pearson/Alamy; P18(B): Derek Latta/Shutterstock; P19: Gilles Paire/Shutterstock; P20(Bgrnd): MartinMaritz/Shutterstock; P20(B): Wlad74/Shutterstock; P21(T): Ventus Innovative Products; P21(BL): TongChuwit/Shutterstock; P21(BR): Berlin Boombox; P22(T): Canadapanda/Shutterstock; P22(B): Christian Bertrand/Shutterstock; P23: Neveshkin Nikolay/Shutterstock; P24(Bgrnd): Olivier Asselin/Alamy; P24(TR): TongChuwit/Shutterstock; P24(BR): Eliza Grinnell/Harvard Seas; P25: Wiklander/Shutterstock; P26: Waldru/Shutterstock; P27(B): Imaginechina/Corbis; P27(T): TongChuwit/Shutterstock; P28: Stringer Shanghai/Reuters; P29(TR): Worldreader; P29(BL): PC Plus Magazine/Getty; P29(BR): TongChuwit/Shutterstock; P30–31: Saicle/Shutterstock; P31(L): Oleksiy Mark/Shutterstock; P31(C): Shutterstock; P31(R): Barone Firenze/Shutterstock.
Index Page: Sergey Nivens/Shutterstock.

Illustration: All-free-downloads.com (P10–11, 14, 18, 19, 21, 22–23).

Printed in Canada/072016/PB20160525

Library and Archives Canada Cataloguing in Publication

Greathead, Helen, author
     My smartphone and other digital accessories / Helen Greathead.

(Well made, fair trade)
Includes index.
Issued in print and electronic formats.
ISBN 978-0-7787-2715-6 (hardback).--
ISBN 978-0-7787-2738-5 (paperback).--ISBN 978-1-4271-1819-6 (html)

     1. Digital electronics--Juvenile literature. 2. Smartphones--Juvenile literature. 3. Ubiquitous computing--Juvenile literature. 4. Digital music players--Juvenile literature. 5. Digital cameras--Juvenile literature. I. Title.

TK7868.D5G744 2016   j621.3845'6   C2016-902581-0
                                                                          C2016-902582-9

Library of Congress Cataloging-in-Publication Data

Names: Greathead, Helen, author.
Title: My smartphone and other digital accessories / Helen Greathead.
Description: St. Catharines, Ontario ; New York, New York : Crabtree Publishing Company, 2017. | Series: Well made, fair trade | "First published in 2014 by Franklin Watts." | Includes index.
Identifiers: LCCN 2016016659 (print) | LCCN 2016016814 (ebook) | ISBN 9780778727156 (reinforced library binding) | ISBN 9780778727385 (pbk.) | ISBN 9781427118196 (electronic HTML)
Subjects: LCSH: Digital electronics--Juvenile literature. | Smartphones--Juvenile literature. | Ubiquitous computing--Juvenile literature. | Digital music players--Juvenile literature. | Digital cameras--Juvenile literature.
Classification: LCC TK7868.D5 G744 2017 (print) | LCC TK7868.D5 (ebook) | DDC 621.3845/6--dc23
LC record available at https://lccn.loc.gov/2016016659

Contents

Smart trade   4

Smartphones   6

Laptops   10

Digital cameras   14

MP3 players and iPods   18

Games consoles   22

Tablets and e-readers   26

Glossary   30

Websites   31

Index   32

Words in **bold** can be found in the glossary on page 30.

Smart trade

The latest smart devices make huge profits for the big electronics companies. However, the miners and factory workers who help produce these devices often work in unsafe conditions and are poorly paid. Fair trade organizations are working together to make producing these products fair for all involved.

Everyone wants to use the latest laptops, smartphones, and tablets.

What are fair trade programs?

The demand for electronic smart devices is growing all the time. Making these devices can provide much-needed work for many people, especially in **developing countries**. Fair trade programs are ways of making sure these workers are paid a fair price for their work. Pressure from customers and fair trade organizations has created fair trade programs that are slowly working to improve the lives of workers and their families.

Explore the issues

This book explains where our electronic devices come from, and explores some of the problems associated with making them. These problems include poor or dangerous working conditions for workers, and the environmental damage that **manufacturing** the products can cause. The book looks at some solutions already in place, explains why fair trade is important, and discusses what you can do to help.

Labeling gadgets

Fair trade food can be labeled to show its origins, but with digital devices it is more difficult. Each device may contain hundreds of parts that are produced and manufactured in many different countries. Because of this, it can be hard to keep track of where every piece is made, and under what conditions. Today, more electronics companies are starting to take responsibility for their **supply chain** as a result of increased pressure from customers.

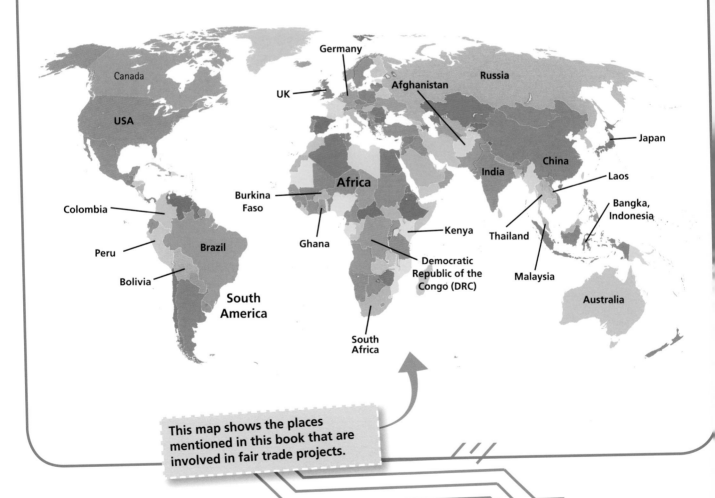

This map shows the places mentioned in this book that are involved in fair trade projects.

Smartphones

Experts estimate there will be 6.1 billion smartphones in use around the world by the end of this decade! China is the biggest market for smartphones—30 million were sold in just one month in 2012. India and the United States are not far behind. Smartphones are expensive, but many people still upgrade their model every 18 months to 2 years.

What is in a smartphone?

There are hundreds of different parts to a smartphone, each made from a wide range of materials, including copper in the wires, gold in the circuit boards, and over 40 different chemical elements. All phones contain around 0.7 ounces (20 g) of tin, which is used to make the **solder** that holds the parts together. The electronics industry uses almost half of all the tin mined today.

Phones are often seen as disposable. In the U.S. alone, about 140 million smart and mobile phones end up in **landfill sites** every year.

Smartphones get their name because of the "clever" features they include, such as a camera and Web browser, and many of the functions of a computer.

Where are smartphones made?

Smartphones travel a long way to reach their customers and many different countries are involved in their production and assembly. For example, the Apple iPhone is designed in North America, while the **microchip** controlling the phone's graphics is designed by Imagination Technologies in the United Kingdom. The gyroscope that lets you use a phone lengthwise or sideways comes from a French-Italian company.

The metals that are used to make an iPhone's components may have been mined in Africa, China, or Indonesia. Finally, the phones are most often assembled in an Asian factory. Eighty-five percent of iPhone 6 phones were assembled in China.

Reuse, recycle

A discarded smartphone takes 1,000 years to break down. To be eco-friendly, it's best to keep the phone you already have, and replace parts if they break. Or if you really want to get rid of your old smartphone, try recycling it—find out about a program near you.

Tin mine trouble

Tin is used in most electronic devices, including smartphones. It is dug out of rocks made of heavy clay or sifted through huge puddles of dirty water. Mining tin is hard and dangerous work. Many tin mines in countries such as Africa and China are not properly equipped or supervised. Health and safety standards for workers are poor or don't exist. Tin miners are expected to work long hours for very little pay. Breathing in tin dust can cause many types of illnesses, from sore eyes and skin problems, to liver and brain damage.

Environmental damage

Poor standards in the mines can also be very harmful to the local environment. Dangerous chemicals can get into the water system and poison the water people drink. **Toxins** can also get into the oceans and kill the fish that provide food for the local people, and destroy healthy coral reefs.

Good buy!

In the eastern Democratic Republic of the Congo (DRC), armed **militia** control the tin mines, sometimes forcing miners to work at gunpoint and terrorizing local villagers. This is why the tin produced here is known as conflict tin. The electronics company Fairphone sources its tin from the Conflict-Free Tin Initiative in the DRC. These mines are carefully monitored and miners are paid a fair price for the tin they produce. Local **cooperatives** buy safety equipment, such as helmets and boots, and make sure the mineshafts are stable. A tracking system means producers can see that their tin has come from a responsibly managed mine.

Fairphone uses conflict-free tin. The phone comes apart easily, so parts can be recycled and replaced.

Case study: Bangka Island tin mines, Indonesia

The tin mines on Bangka Island are dangerous places to work. On average in 2011, one miner died every week due to work-related accidents or illness. Some are buried alive when there is a landslide. But the pay is better than at other mines — about $7 a day. This money helps the local people to pay for things they could not otherwise afford, such as sending their children to school.

Buried alive

In 2012, a miner named Suge was buried in a landslide at a tin mine. Suge was one of the lucky ones. He was dug out alive and survived with just a broken arm and leg. His boss promised to pay him some compensation, and said that Suge could have his job back when he recovered. In most mines, there is no compensation for injured workers, and no job waiting for them when they have healed.

Poor working and environmental standards in the mines are destroying forests, beaches, and farms, and ruining Bangka's tourist trade. While tin still makes money for local people today, the island's future does not look very bright.

A mine worker at a Bangka Island tin mine. Every year over 900,000 tons of tin are extracted from mines in Indonesia.

Laptops

Laptops are more convenient and portable than a desktop computer, and use around 25 percent less energy. But do you know what's inside your laptop?

What materials are in a laptop?

Up to 50 percent of your laptop is made up of as many as 20 different types of metals, including lead, copper, and mercury. Coltan is also an essential ingredient. It is a metallic **ore** that can hold a very high electrical charge, which stops a laptop from overheating.

Since 2008, more laptops have been sold worldwide than personal computers.

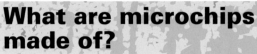

What are microchips made of?

There are thousands of parts inside a laptop, including a microchip. This tiny piece goes through hundreds of stages of manufacture, including treatment with toxic chemicals and gases so that it can conduct electricity. Microchips are made from silica, which comes from a type of sand found in Brazil. It is refined in Germany, converted to **polysilicon** in Japan, turned into a super-thin plate in the U.S., and made into microchips in Malaysia. Finally, the chips find their way onto a **circuit board** in China.

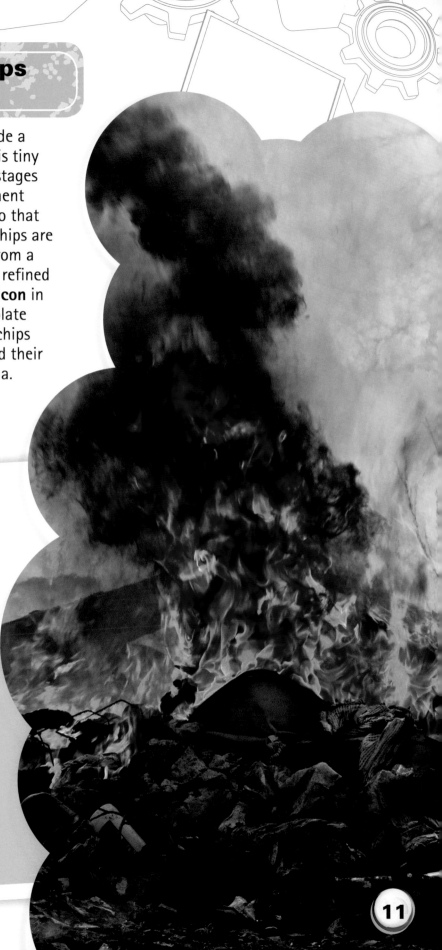

Reuse, recycle

In some countries, **e-waste** is often burned in landfill sites, and dangerous smoke fills the air. To help stop this, you can recycle your laptop through a local program. Some online companies will collect unwanted computers and recycle them for charity. Call your city or town hall and ask about recycling options.

Case study: Coltan mine, Democratic Republic of the Congo, Africa

Some people call coltan "black gold," because it has brought wealth to a very poor region of Africa. However, most miners have no idea where their coltan will end up, or how much it is really worth. In some mines, workers earn up to $43 U.S. a week from coltan. In other mines, young children such as 10-year-old Eudes have been forced to give up school to work in the mine, earning just over $1 a day. The work is hard and dull. Eudes has to dig in the mud, rinsing earth from the mineral deposits he finds. He doesn't have any safety equipment. Eudes also fears that soldiers, who control the mine, will come and take his money or his coltan to buy weapons.

Good buy!

No laptops can yet claim to be 100 percent fair trade, but a German company called Nager-IT has been working on a fair trade mouse. It uses components from mines that do not use child labor, and where workers are paid fair wages, health and safety measures are enforced, and **human rights** are recognized.

It can take Eudes several days to mine just a few ounces of coltan.

Conflict-free coltan

A terrible **civil war** in the DRC ended in 2003, but rebel soldiers are still active, and they sometimes fight and kill to take control of the precious coltan mines. As a result, coltan has become known as a conflict mineral. The Solutions for Hope project was set up in 2011 by the American company Motorola Solutions. Its aim is to make sure that conflict-free mines sell their coltan directly to a cooperative whose labor practices are watched closely. The cooperative then prepares the laptop components for Motorola. That way, Motorola knows where the coltan comes from and can label it conflict-free.

Environment matters

Polystyrene packaging is made from oil, which is hard to recycle and takes years to break down. It also pollutes the oceans. Dell, a computer manufacturer, now sells its laptops in protective packaging made from **sustainable** bamboo.

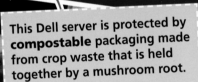

This Dell server is protected by **compostable** packaging made from crop waste that is held together by a mushroom root.

The DRC's gorilla population has fallen by 90 percent, and they are now seriously endangered.

Endangered gorillas

Huge areas of rain forest in the DRC have been cleared to make way for coltan mines. People moving to find work in the mines chop down trees for fuel, and eat **bushmeat**, such as gorillas. Kemet, the world's largest producer of coltan used in laptops, has asked its supply chains to make sure that the coltan they supply is conflict-free. In the United States, campaigns encourage the recycling of e-waste to provide an alternative source of coltan. Both programs may help to protect the DRC gorillas.

62mm 1:1.4

Digital cameras

The first photograph was developed in 1827, and since then billions of photographs have been taken. At least 30 million photos are uploaded to Facebook every day.

Where are cameras made?

A camera can contain more than 180 parts. **Raw materials** are shipped from around the world to the factories where the cameras are put together. Camera companies often have their products assembled in south-east Asian countries such as Thailand, China, and Laos, where lower wages make them cheaper to produce.

Selfies are used for Facebook, blogs, and to share with friends.

How is the lens made?

Special optical glass starts off as a powder made up of hundreds of raw materials, such as plastic, rubber, and steel. The powder is heated, melted, cut, and shaped to make the lens. Both sides of the lens go through several stages of polishing. Finally, a thin film is applied to the finished lens to stop light reflection.

What special conditions are needed?

Conditions in the camera factories have to be just right. The lens, for example, needs to be polished, washed, and inspected many times. The factory has clean rooms where all workers wear masks, gloves, and special protective clothing. One tiny speck of dust can affect how well the lens works.

This factory worker wears special clothing to prevent dust from damaging the lens of the CCTV camera.

Difficult market for cameras

Cameras take time to produce and can be expensive to make, yet **consumers** expect high-quality cameras at cheap prices. Today, digital cameras are competing with smartphones that have built-in cameras, so manufacturers have to keep costs down to make their product more appealing.

Case study: Tianjin camera factory, China

Compared to many factories in the area, the Tianjin camera factory offers good working conditions.

Zhao is 19 and works 12-hour shifts as a camera inspector. She doesn't have to travel far to get to work as she lives in a dormitory at the factory, which is common in China. The dorms in Tianjin are clean and air-conditioned. With overtime, Zhao can earn between $280 and $550 U.S. a month, which is more than the neighboring factories pay.

Reuse, recycle

Never throw an old camera in the trash. Toxins inside it are dangerous for the environment. For older digital cameras, spare parts can be hard to come by, so try taking it to a photography store instead. Or you could help a charity by donating your old camera to them.

The Tianjin factory's 50,000 employees assemble mobile phones, TVs, CCTV cameras, and digital cameras. Assembly line workers put together 200 to 300 camera lenses each day.

Some specialty camera stores may be happy to buy your old camera.

Hard labor in the factories

China Labor Watch is a **not-for-profit organization** that works with others to assess the conditions in China's digital camera factories. It has reported that in some factories, workers were not paid for their overtime, they were forced to work long hours without a break, and they got into serious trouble if they did not work fast enough. In most factories, there was no one to complain to, and workers were not allowed to join a **union**.

As a result of the report, one manufacturer, Samsung, set up a plan that improves working conditions. They agreed to ensure that the factories they used to create the parts for their electronic goods followed local labor laws, as well as Samsung's own employment policies.

Good buy!

Nokia was voted the most **sustainable** company in the world in 2010, by the independent environmental organization Greenpeace, in its Green Electronics Guide. Nokia says it aims to track supply chains and ethically source the materials used in its products. Nokia builds its factories close to where its products will be sold and continues to use a high percentage of **renewable energy.** Caring for the environment is a high priority.

Nokia was the first company to produce a phone with a built-in camera.

Environment matters

Digital cameras guzzle batteries like no other device. Batteries are bad for the environment. They contain dangerous chemicals that can contaminate the ground, water systems, and the air if they are not disposed of properly. If you buy a new camera, make sure it has rechargeable batteries.

MP3 players and iPods

Portable music players, such as MP3 players and iPods, were developed so that whole music collections could be stored on one tiny device.

What is an MP3 player made of?

As with all electronic devices, an MP3 player is made from a wide range of materials, including silicon, liquid crystals, plastic, and precious metals, which can include gold, silver, and platinum.

Portable music players have changed the way we listen to music.

Workers in an open-pit mine in Burkina Faso, West Africa. The best way to mine gold is to create an underground shaft, but this is expensive and can take a long time.

Where does the gold come from?

Gold is used in MP3 players to make electric switches and connect wires. Around the world, there are several hundred gold mines, but just 20 countries produce three quarters of the world's gold. In 2013, the top producers were China, Australia, and the United States. Gold is difficult to find, and it takes about 3,000 tons (2,722 metric tons) of rock to produce just 22 to 33 pounds (10 to 15 kg) of gold. The environmental group Friends of the Earth claims that you could find more gold in a ton of cell phones than in a ton of rock from a gold mine.

Dirty gold mining

Many gold mines around the world are open-pit mines. This means that explosives are used to blast the rock to reach the gold. This is a dirty gold mining practice that destroys huge areas of the environment.

Another dirty gold mining practice is heap leaching. Rocks are heaped up and sprayed with a deadly chemical called cyanide, which sticks to the gold. The cyanide soaks into the ground, where it pollutes the soil and poisons the water supply. Some mines use a liquid metal called mercury to find gold. Mercury fumes are deadly for wildlife and humans, and can damage the liver, brains, and lungs.

Case study: Driefontein Mine, South Africa

In September 2013, 80,000 gold miners at the Driefontein mine went on strike for better wages, even though it meant they would earn no money while being on strike.

Albertina, a miner, starts work at 3:45 a.m., and has to work deep under the ground, where the heat is unbearable. Her shift lasts eight hours and during that time, miners work bent over in the cramped tunnels. But conditions are better than they used to be. There are fewer accidents, the workers get breaks for fresh air, and there are fans to protect them from the heat. However, Albertina takes home only about $438 U.S. per month in wages, which is not enough to feed her family.

Struggling industry

Strikes are continuing at South Africa's gold mines, and the gold industry is struggling. The lack of production is putting pressure on the economy. It is estimated that every day of a strike costs the country $32 million U.S. Mining companies say they cannot afford to pay the wages the miners are demanding.

The headgear at the top of the mineshaft hauls minerals up from deep underground.

Gold ore: about 40 percent of the world's gold ore is mined in South Africa.

Fairtrade gold

Fairtrade gold was launched in 2011 in Peru, Bolivia, and Colombia. Fairtrade miners respect the environment and follow safe working practices. They are paid a fair minimum price for their gold, and given $1,736 U.S. per pound on top of their pay for local improvement projects. In the Sotrami community in Peru, after less than two years of mining Fairtrade gold, the community was able to open a grocery store, improve the local health and dental care services, and clean up the water supply.

Good buy!

Instead of having a plug, the Spin Eco media player has a handle so you can wind it up. One minute of winding provides 45 minutes of sound and visual display. Once it's fully charged, this device will keep playing for 55 hours. You can also use it to view photos and videos, store up to 2,000 songs, and even recharge your phone.

At the end of the product's working life, the Spin Eco media player can be recycled.

Reuse, recycle

When it comes to using your Iphone, Ipod, or MP3 player with speakers, connecting it to a Berlin Boombox is a brilliant eco-option. The Boombox comes in a do-it-yourself cardboard package that turns into an eco-speaker, with just a few electronic parts.

This brown Boombox is 100 percent recyclable.

Game consoles

The first home video game that could be connected to a television was launched in 1972. Today, millions of homes worldwide have a game console.

When the new Xbox One was launched in 13 countries in 2013, 1 million units were sold in just 24 hours.

What is in a game console?

Among the many components of a game console is a **multi-core processor**, which holds several processors on one chip. The processor controls the functions of the console, such as the graphics and the sound. In 2008, Greenpeace took apart a number of game consoles from different manufacturers, and found several toxic chemicals inside. One chemical—polyvinyl chloride, or PVC—is used to coat cables and wires, while other chemicals are used to stop the gadget from catching fire.

Are these chemicals dangerous?

Children's toys are checked carefully for dangerous materials, but computers and game consoles are not considered toys. If they were, children would be banned from using them in some parts of the world.

The greatest dangers are faced by the workers who assemble computers and game consoles, due to the chemical fumes they are exposed to while working. Good **ventilation** and protection from the fumes is essential to keep workers healthy.

A 2008 report showed that some workers in game console factories in China became ill after inhaling toxic fumes. Some workers needed to be hospitalized, even though they were wearing masks and the factory ventilation met health standards.

Future damage

If you don't dispose of your console carefully, the chemicals inside could become part of the growing mountain of e-waste.

Although most e-waste is now 100 percent recyclable, some still finds its way to countries such as China, India, and Russia. Instead of recycling old electronic equipment, these countries often burn it, which creates toxic fumes. Children living in these areas have higher levels of toxins in their blood.

Most consoles use huge amounts of energy. A lot of electrical power is required to play 3-D games, to watch a video through your console, and to use the console with your TV screen.

Case study: e-waste mountains, Ghana, Africa

The dumping of e-waste is illegal, but container ships still arrive in the port of Ghana's capital city, Accra, full of old electronics. Most of these devices are useless, and end up dumped in scrap markets. Families often send their children to Accra to work in the scrap markets. Here, children as young as 8 spend 12 hours a day sifting through piles of electronic waste, looking for copper and aluminium to sell for money. Using their bare hands, the children burn the plastic around wires to get at the metal inside. This creates toxic black fumes that are extremely harmful to the children's health.

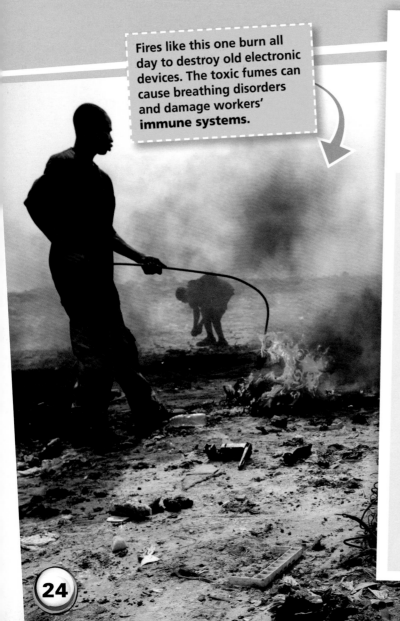

Fires like this one burn all day to destroy old electronic devices. The toxic fumes can cause breathing disorders and damage workers' immune systems.

Reuse, recycle

After reading about the e-waste problems in Ghana, American engineering student Rachel Field came up with a simple idea she calls the Bicyclean. A **stationary** bicycle uses a pedal-powered grinding wheel to break up electronic waste. The waste is caught in a box, along with any harmful dust, and all the materials can then be recycled.

Taking responsibility

The environmental group Greenpeace alerted the world to the problem of e-waste in India in 2005. Since then, Indian electronics producers have been encouraged to ban toxic substances from their products. In 2011, new laws were passed to make companies responsible for the e-waste their goods will eventually produce.

A new program in Kenya, sponsored by computer giant Dell, has helped 27 women who once collected waste from scrap heaps. The women have been trained and given loans so they can buy and sort e-waste to resell at Kenya's brand-new e-waste recycling center. The workers are given a fair price for their work, and no longer have to put their health at risk.

Environment matters

Your computer monitor accounts for about one third of the electricity your computer uses. Switch off your computer when not in use, or at least make sure it is in sleep mode, with screensavers turned off.

By 2020, electronic companies will have recycled around 2 billion pounds (907 million kg) of electronic devices at the Kenya e-waste center.

Tablets and e-readers

E-readers first became available in 1998, and the introduction of the tablet soon followed. Millions are sold every year, and many users upgrade to the latest model as soon as it is available.

What is in your tablet?

All of today's tablets contain **rare earth minerals**. There are 17 different types of rare earth minerals, and they come in a powdered form. They are expensive, but without them your tablet would probably not exist. Rare earth minerals are in the magnets that keep your device small and working fast. They are also responsible for the colors in your screen, the touchscreen element, and even the polish that makes your tablet shine.

A tablet lets you read a book, watch a movie, or talk to a friend on Skype. You can do everything on just one device.

Where do rare earth minerals come from?

Rare earth minerals can be found all over the world, but they are difficult to **excavate.** China is the main producer of the minerals, but it has cut back on sales to the rest of the world due to environmental concerns (see page 28). Now other countries are scrambling to find new supplies or alternative materials. Excavations are underway in Bolivia and Afghanistan.

Mining hazards

Extracting and processing rare earth minerals can damage the environment if not done properly. The minerals are often found with **radioactive** elements and if these are not monitored and controlled, they can enter the ground, water systems, and the air.

Reuse, recycle

Japan has no rare earth minerals of its own, but is planning to produce 300,000 tons of rare earth metals by recycling components from its e-waste mountain.

A rare earth mine in South-west China. In 2010, China produced 95 percent of the world's rare earth minerals.

Case study: Baotou, Inner Mongolia, China

Li Guirong was born in a village near Baotou in the 1940s. He remembers the time when there were fields full of fruit and vegetables in the area. Gradually, pollution from local industries caused the crops to die, and now nothing can grow. Today, a dam of dirty water covers 6.3 miles (10 km) of land. There is no life in the water. Instead it is polluted with waste from rare earth mineral processing and from other factories in the area. The chemicals that are used to extract rare earth minerals and radioactive material can cause several types of cancer. Water from the dam has already polluted the **groundwater** in the area and is moving toward the Yellow River, which provides drinking water for most of Northern China.

Ghost village

Ten years ago, 2,000 people lived in Li's village. Many have moved away, and now there are just 300 people left. The Chinese government is at last taking notice of the environmental problems that rare earth mining is causing. Billions of dollars are now being spent in an attempt to clean up the environment, and rare earth mineral exports have been limited.

Workers at Baotou, China's largest rare earth mine. When China limited rare earth exports, prices for the minerals skyrocketed.

Getting better?

Many different organizations monitor the ethical and environmental performance of the electronic devices we use. They assess the sourcing of the device's materials, treatment of workers, the environmental impact of the device, and its energy consumption. By making this information public, consumers can be aware of where and how their electronic devices are produced. This puts pressure on companies to increase and improve their environmental and fair trade practices.

The Ethical Consumer magazine examined a range of tablets to determine which were the most ethically produced. The winner was the Archos Internet tablet, which scored just 10 points out of a possible 20. There is still a long way to go, but at least people are thinking of ways to improve the manufacturing process of our electronic devices.

Tablets have helped people in many ways. Organizations such as Worldreader are helping to improve literacy skills in Africa by replacing out-of-date school books with e-readers.

Reuse, recycle

The Ellen MacArthur Foundation believes that all electronic products should be "made to be made again." They call their plan the circular economy. First, electronic products are designed to not produce waste. They are made using renewable energy and without any hazardous chemicals. Second, no one ever buys an electronic product—instead, they only rent it. Then, at the end of the product's working life, it is taken back to the rental company to be recycled, and no hazardous e-waste is ever created.

The Archos Internet tablet

Glossary

bushmeat   Meat from wild game such as chimpanzees, lions, and gorillas

circuit board   A piece of electrical equipment that makes a computer work

civil war   A war between citizens of the same country

compostable   Biodegradable, or rots easily and quickly

consumers   People who buy or use goods and services

cooperatives   When people or groups work together so that everyone benefits

developing countries   Countries that are economically poor and have a less developed industrial base compared to other countries

e-waste (electronic waste)   All discarded electronic devices and equipment

excavate   Dig out or remove from the earth

groundwater   Water that is in the ground, just beneath the surface

human rights   Basic rights, such as being safe, free, and being able to look after yourself and your family

immune system   The system of organs, tissues, and cells that protect the body from infection

landfill sites   Deep pits used to bury waste

manufacturing   Make, usually in a factory

microchip   A tiny piece of silicon able to hold millions of circuits

militia   Rebel soldiers who are not supported by a government

multi-core processor   Several processors combined onto one chip, which increases computing possibilities and saves energy

not-for-profit organization   A company that operates without a making a profit

ore   Rock containing a combination of minerals, including metals such as iron or gold, that occurs naturally in the ground

polysilicon   A material made up of many silicon crystals. Silicon is a substance that is found naturally in the earth.

radioactive   Rays or particles from nuclear waste that can cause illness or death

rare earth minerals   A collection of 17 minerals found naturally in the ground that are used in electronic devices

raw materials   Basic materials, such as coal and wood, before they are manufactured

renewable energy   A source of energy that occurs naturally and will never run out, such as solar, wave, or wind energy

solder   Join two metals together with heat

stationary   Does not move

supply chain   The journey a product goes through, from sourcing of materials to finished product reaching the customer

sustainable   Something that can be kept going or maintained in the future without damaging the environment or its resources

toxins   Dangerous substances that can harm humans, animals, and the environment

union   An organization of workers who join together to protect the rights and interests of its members

ventilation   A way of keeping the air fresh by taking out stale or toxic air and replacing with clean air

Websites

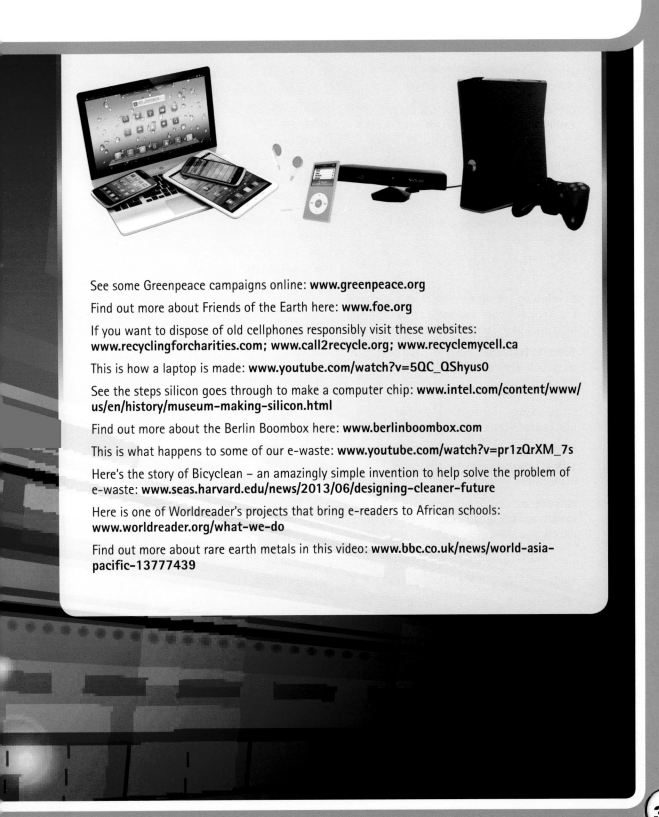

See some Greenpeace campaigns online: **www.greenpeace.org**

Find out more about Friends of the Earth here: **www.foe.org**

If you want to dispose of old cellphones responsibly visit these websites:
www.recyclingforcharities.com; www.call2recycle.org; www.recyclemycell.ca

This is how a laptop is made: **www.youtube.com/watch?v=5QC_QShyus0**

See the steps silicon goes through to make a computer chip: **www.intel.com/content/www/us/en/history/museum-making-silicon.html**

Find out more about the Berlin Boombox here: **www.berlinboombox.com**

This is what happens to some of our e-waste: **www.youtube.com/watch?v=pr1zQrXM_7s**

Here's the story of Bicyclean – an amazingly simple invention to help solve the problem of e-waste: **www.seas.harvard.edu/news/2013/06/designing-cleaner-future**

Here is one of Worldreader's projects that bring e-readers to African schools: **www.worldreader.org/what-we-do**

Find out more about rare earth metals in this video: **www.bbc.co.uk/news/world-asia-pacific-13777439**

Index

Afghanistan 5, 27
Africa 5, 7, 8, 9, 23, 27, 28
Archos Internet tablet 29
Asia 5, 7, 14
Australia 5, 19

batteries 17
Berlin Boombox 21
Bicyclean 24
Bolivia 5, 21, 27
Brazil 5, 11
Burkina Faso 5, 19

China 5, 6, 7, 8, 11, 14, 16, 17, 19,
   23, 27, 28
Colombia 5, 21
coltan 10, 12-13
computer mouse 12
conflict-free sources 8, 13
cooperatives 8
cyanide 19

Dell 13, 25
Democratic Republic
   of the Congo (DRC) 5, 8, 12, 13
digital cameras 14-17
Driefontein mine 20

e-readers 26-29
e-waste 11, 23, 24, 25
Ellen MacArthur Foundation 29
environmental damage 8, 9, 13, 17,
   19, 27, 28

Facebook 14
Fairphone 8
Fairtrade Foundation 4

game consoles 22-25
Germany 5, 11, 12
Ghana 5, 24
gold 19, 20, 21
gorillas 13
Greenpeace 17, 22, 25
Guirong, Li 28

India 6, 23, 25
Indonesia 5, 9
iPhones 7
iPods 18-21

Japan 5, 11, 27

Kenya 5, 25

labelling devices 5
landslides 9
Laos 5, 14
laptops 10-13

Malaysia 11
map 5
microchips 7, 11, 22
mining 7, 9, 12, 13, 19, 20, 27, 28
Motorola 13
MP3 players 18-21

Nokia 17

packaging 13
Peru 5, 21

rain forests 13
rare earth minerals 26, 27
recycling 7, 8, 11,13,16, 21, 24, 25,
   27, 29
renewable energy 17, 29
Russia 23

Samsung 17
smartphones 6-9
South Africa 5, 20
Spin Ecomedia player 21

tablets 26-29
Thailand 5, 14
tin 6, 8-9
toxic chemicals 22, 28
toxic fumes 23, 24
toxins 8, 11, 16, 23

United States 5, 6, 11, 19